Kids l...
Choose Your...

"These boo...
Sometimes the choice seems like it
will solve everything, but you wonder
if it's a trap."

Matt Harmon, age 11

"I think you'd call this a book for active
readers, and I am definitely an
active reader!"

Ava Kendrick, age 11

"You decide your own fate,
but your fate is still a surprise."

Chun Tao Lin, age 10

"Come on in this book if you're crazy
enough! One wrong move and
you're a goner!"

Ben Curley, age 9

"You can read *Choose Your Own
Adventure* books so many wonderful
ways. You could go find your dog
or follow a unicorn."

Celia Lawton, age 11

THE TRAIL OF LOST TIME

BY R.A. MONTGOMERY

ILLUSTRATED BY VLADIMIR SEMIONOV
COVER ILLUSTRATED BY GABHOR UTOMO

CHOOSECO
WAITSFIELD, VERMONT

Illustrated by: Vladimir Semionov
Cover Art by: Gabhor Utomo
Book Design: Jamie Proctor-Brassard of Letter10 Creative

For information regarding permission, write to:

CHOOSECO®

P.O. Box 46
Waitsfield, Vermont 05673
www.cyoa.com

ISBN-13: 978-1937133-03-0
ISBN-10: 1-937133-03-6

Published simultaneously in the United States and Canada

Printed in Canada

0 9 8 7 6 5 4 3 2 1

This book is dedicated to Ramsey.

BEWARE and WARNING!

This book is different from other books.

You and YOU ALONE are in charge of what happens in this story.

There are dangers, choices, adventures, and consequences. YOU must use all of your numerous talents and much of your enormous intelligence. The wrong decision could end in disaster—even death. But, don't despair. At any time, YOU can go back and make another choice, alter the path of your story, and change its result.

When your famous archeologist grandfather passes away, he leaves your parents his ranch in New Mexico. But you get something he thinks is even more valuable: a map to an ancient kiva located deep on the ranch that lets you travel back in time. Shall you touch the kokopelli image to travel to the time and lands of the Anazsazi? Where will the dugout canoe take you? Do you dare access the time and place when the wooly mammoth walked the earth? The map has unlimited possibilities, but no instructions. Be brave and curious, but be careful—will you live to return to your own present time?

You stare at the envelope with your name written in faded ink. The lawyer handed it to you an hour ago after he read your grandfather's will. Your grandfather, Jasper Ambergris, was a world-famous archaeologist. He left the ranch in New Mexico to your parents where you spend every summer. He left you some stocks and bonds to pay for college. Last of all, he left you the envelope you are looking at. The lawyer said something very strange when he handed it to you: "Your grandfather said that what was in this envelope was the most valuable thing of all."

Then he gave you a wink.

Turn to the next page.

Your mind drifts back four years, when you and your grandfather were digging near a *midden*, or garbage heap, about a half mile from the old adobe house where he lived. You were only eight then. You remember the rocky, dry, reddish soil, the desert plants, a few flowers, and the scrub pinion dotting the rough hillside. That was when you saw it flash in the sunlight, something white and shiny.

What is that? you wondered. You brushed the red dirt away quickly.

A skull! You found a fossilized skull.

It was when you touched the skull that something really strange happened.

Go on to the next page.

"What have you got there?" your grandfather asked.

You gave him the strangest look as the words tumbled into your head.

"This is the fossilized skull of an Anasazi Paleo-Indian. Carbon dating and DNA sampling will most probably reveal it is 2,200 years old, male, aged around late teens, died of wounds from hunting prototype bison."

You grandfather raised his eyebrows, smiled, and nodded.

"So you have the gift," he said, sounding impressed. "I was wondering if anyone else in the family would inherit it. You see, no one knows this. Not even your parents. But whenever I make a new find, a pot or a basket, well, all I have to do is touch it and somehow I know how old it is and where it came from."

"Does that mean you'll tell me what's in the hidden canyon at the far end of the ranch?"

Turn to the next page.

Your grandfather just smiled. "One day I will. Just be patient."

You glance down now at your grandfather's envelope. He told the lawyer than it contained the most valuable thing he owned. Does it contain clues to the location of the ancient boxed canyon that was kept secret and off limits?

"To be honest, I don't think it actually exists," your dad said one day when you asked. "Those stories about people disappearing into the canyon are just rumors."

People disappearing? You rip open the envelope.

Go on to the next page.

My Dear Child,

When I was a young man studying for my archaeology degree, I had a vivid dream. In it, I entered a narrow gorge no wider than a man. The gorge led to a round room carved out of rock but open to the sky. Once inside, I could travel to many places in time, even back before human habitation on planet Earth. I realized that the room was a kiva, the kind used by the Pueblo Indians as a place of ceremony. And this dream kiva was a kind of wormhole to the past! Years later on a dig here in New Mexico, I came face-to-face with the same narrow gorge. Except this time it was real. The entrance to the space was between two tall rocks, and nearly invisible. The gorge twisted and turned and finally led onto the same ancient kiva open to the sky. Thus below, I give you my most precious possession. It is a drawing of the canyon entrance. And a map that will take you there. Once inside, follow the trail to the second left after the first right. Upon entering the kiva, look for the ancient map carved into the sandstone. Study it closely before choosing. You must feel your way, and it will guide you well. If you pay close attention, it will lead you home. Good luck!

Much love,
Grandpa Jasper

Turn to the next page.

You find your mom in the kitchen making dinner. Her eyes are red from crying, but you pretend not to notice.

"I'm going out for a walk," you say.

"That's fine, but be home in an hour," she says, "or you'll be late for dinner."

"Right," you nod, taking off out the back door. You quickly hike past the horse paddocks and the old barn. You glance at the diagram in the letter and take the winding trail into the hills. A short while later, less than a half mile from the house, you come upon the canyon entrance, just as your grandfather drew it. You have passed this way a million times, but you have never seen it before now!

Do you have time to go inside to investigate? Or should you wait and start fresh tomorrow?

If you decide to investigate right away, go on to the next page.

If you decide to go home for dinner, and come back first thing in the morning, turn to page 9.

You look at your watch. There are still forty minutes until dinner. It can't hurt to take a quick look inside. At least you can begin to look for the carved map your grandfather wrote about.

You slip between the two nondescript boulders into the narrow canyon. There is just enough room to get by. You can easily touch both sides of the canyon wall. After 100 feet or so, you come to a fork. You flick on your LED mini-flashlight. You reread the letter. Your grandfather said to take "the second left after the first right." This must be the first right, so you take it. Several seconds later, there is a fork to the left but you walk straight. When you reach the second left, the air suddenly grows cooler. Overhead the canyon opening to the mesa above is less than two feet wide. It feels like you are descending lower as you move ahead. Suddenly you turn a final corner and stumble into a round space, carved in the rock, the sacred kiva your grandfather wrote about. It's no more than 25 feet across. But it's at least 75 feet to the opening above. You scan the entire circle, carefully panning the flashlight's beam across the stone. There it is! The map carved into the wall.

Turn to page 10.

You decide to put off investigating the canyon and kiva until morning. The sun is starting to set, and it will be dark soon. As you hike toward the lights of home, you notice a huge dark storm system coming in from the west.

Dinner is quiet. You tell your parents you are tucking in early, that you plan to go digging tomorrow in the cliffs nearby. Which is more or less true.

That night there is an enormous rainstorm. Normally these cloudbursts last only twenty or thirty minutes. But this one goes on for hours.

When you wake up, the sky is blue and everything looks clean and fresh. But when you reach the opening of the narrow canyon, it has disappeared under a mudslide.

For years you search for the canyon, but you never find it. Your chance to travel the Trail of Lost Time has vanished.

The End

You approach the petroglyph map. The sandstone is old and the carving is faint. It seems like a random mix of different ancient icons: a wooly mammoth, some small dugout canoes, the flute player Kokopelli who looks like an ant playing the flute. And a large spider. There are also some large uneven shapes that are connected by a thin strip near the very top. You stare some more. Something about the shapes seems familiar. Then it dawns on you: It's a map of the world.

The blotch to the left, or west, is the Asian land mass. The shape to the east is the continent of North America. It seems to go as far south as Guatemala, or maybe Colombia. And the thin thread connecting the two continents must be the Bering Strait! During the last ice age 10,000 years ago, sea levels fell so low that a land bridge appeared between the two continents. And people traveled across.

Your grandfather was right about one thing. This map is very, very old.

You continue to study it. There is one icon you don't understand, a spiral. It appears three times.

Go on to the next page.

Now what? You look around. Where is the entrance? You feel a surge of panic. You came in from the opposite side of the kiva. If that's what this is. But the opening from the narrow gorge is gone! And unlike a real kiva, there is no ladder to the top. How do you get out? Is that a door over to your left? You take deep breaths and try to stay calm. You open your grandfather's letter.

"You must feel your way..." he says. "Feel"? What can he mean?

Does he mean that you should touch the carving?

It's now dark and way past dinnertime. But you don't know what else to do.

If you touch the mammoth, turn to page 13.

If you touch the flute player called Kokopelli, turn to page 39.

If you touch the small log raft, turn to page 57.

You reach out nervously and touch the wooly mammoth. As your fingers touch the rough stone, everything goes dark. You feel yourself falling through space until you land with a thump. You shake your head and look around as things come into focus. You are lying in the tundra. As you stand up, all you can see are rolling hills covered in the arctic grasses stretching miles in the distance. It's bordered by a mountain of white ice to the west.

"Where have you been?" a voice behind you demands. "We've been looking for you everywhere. We were about to leave you behind. Are you afraid to hunt the mammoth? If you are, you can stay behind and help the old ones with the young children."

Turn to the next page.

You whirl around and face a young boy, who looks about thirteen. He is covered in animal skins, and wears a skin tied around his head like a scarf. He is holding a spear tipped with sharp flint. He obviously knows you well.

He is not speaking English. But when you open your mouth to reply, neither are you. How do you know this odd language?

If you say, "I am feeling unwell, so I will stay behind for now with the old ones and children," go on to the next page.

If you say, "I am sorry to delay everyone, but I am ready to leave on the hunt," turn to page 28.

"You don't look well," your young companion says. "You look pale. Come on."

You run after the boy with the spear. Less than half a mile away, you come to camp. There is a fire in a circle of rocks. Some young children play nearby. The location is sheltered from the prevailing wind by a hillock. But it also affords a wide view of the surrounding area. You guess that this is so predators, both animal and human, can be seen from far off. There are seven or eight crude lean-to shelters. Some wolf pups cavort with the small children. You remember reading somewhere that wolves were the predecessors of all modern North American dog breeds. They are certainly acting tame.

As you jog into the camp, the adults, men and women both, nod hello. The boy joins them and explains that you have decided to stay behind.

"Where is Isma?" one woman asks.

"She has gone to the river for water," an old man replies. "She will be back in moments."

This reply acts as a signal. The adults turn and begin to trot as a group toward the far hills. You sit down next to an old woman with long silver hair who is sewing animal skins together.

Turn to the next page.

The band of hunting adults is soon a speck on the horizon. You watch the old woman skillfully thread sinew back and forth, creating a blanket from several small matched rabbit skins. Her needle looks like it is made from bone. She keeps looking at the sun overhead.

"Where is that Isma?" she asks, exasperated. "She has been gone for three leks. A trip to the water should take no more than two leks."

The old woman glances at you. "Would you mind going to look for her?"

You look around at the children playing. Aside from two very old men who are dozing in lean-tos, you are the oldest one there.

"Is it safe for me to leave you alone?" you ask.

The old woman smiles. "The Great Spirit has blessed me this far. I suppose he will bless me for another lek."

For some reason, you sense danger. You scan the horizon in every direction. But there is nothing there.

If you decide to go search for Isma, turn to page 18.

If you decide it's wiser to stay with the group, turn to page 24.

"Something is wrong!" she announces. "Why did the fire go out?"

She starts to run, and you try to run after her. But the water slows you down. You look for a place to put the water down. You realize that if you do, most of the water, and all of your and Isma's effort, will drain away.

If you stumble along as fast as you can but keep the water on your head, turn to page 21.

If you put the water down, and run after Isma, turn to page 22.

"Okay, grandmother," you say. "I will find Isma and return soon."

The old woman smiles and nods her approval. You grab a spear from a pile next to the middle lean-to, and head east. How you know where to go, and why you speak and understand this ancient lost language are both mysteries to you. It must have something to do with the wormhole, you think.

You walk briskly. Soon the camp is out of sight, except for a thin wisp of smoke curling into the air. You follow the faint path. About a half hour later, you finally come upon a young girl, no more than ten, struggling with two large animal skins of water, balanced on either end of a pole she has balanced on her head.

"Here," you say, reaching out. "You are carrying too much for your size. I will take that."

When you hoist the pole on to your head, careful to balance it on a small bundle of animal skin, you can hardly believe this thin young girl made it this far.

"It will be enough for the whole evening," she announces proudly. "No one will need to search for water tonight."

You begin the trip back to camp. It is slow going with the heavy water. Isma leads the way and stops suddenly, listening.

"What?" you ask, straining to hear.

Turn to page 17.

Isma soon disappears into the arctic tundra grasses. You follow her as quickly as you can, but the water slows you down. Your legs and arms ache from the weight. You look up, and realize you have lost your way.

"Isma!" you yell. But nothing but the winds through the grass answers your call. You trudge forward. Rivulets of sweat pour down your face. You walk and walk. You should have reached the camp long ago. It's getting dark and colder. You climb to the highest hill and look in every direction. But you see nothing, neither smoke nor light from a fire. You decide to wait until dark, hoping the light of the fire will lead the way.

It is the last you are seen of or heard from.

The End

You decide to leave the water and stay with Isma. The two of you run as fast as your legs can go back to the camp. She knows the way and discerns paths that are invisible to you. But despite your speed, it is too late. When you crest the final hill, Isma yells out in horror.

"Aaiieeeeeyah!" she cries, her eyes filled with tears.

"What happened?" you whisper, looking at the wrecked camp.

You both run forward. The two old men are sprawled facedown at the far edge of the camp, with huge gashes across their backs. The old woman is just behind them, lying faceup, her eyes staring at the darkening sky overhead. Her right arm has been bitten off at the elbow.

"Sloth," Isma whispers. "It was an attack by a sloth."

Go on to the next page.

Just then a small head rises from the grasses about fifty feet away.

"Isma?" he cries.

Suddenly seven more heads pop up. The children run toward you and leap into your arms and grasp your sides. Finally, one of the little girls speaks.

"The giant sloth came right after you left. Grandmother told us to hide in the far switch grass."

"We will need to join the hunters," Isma announces. "It is not safe to stay here. We will come back to bury the elders tomorrow."

Grabbing some dried meat and fresh onions for your journey, and a few small satchels of water, you and Isma collect the small children and head south. You hope you will find the hunters soon.

The End

"Grandmother, Isma is always late," you say. "I would rather stay here."

"Okay," she replies. "You are right. But if that girl did not have her head attached, she would lose it. That is the kind of girl she is."

You don't mention your sense of unease keeping you back. You keep scanning the horizon to the south and west. But there is nothing. The children have progressed to a kind of kickball game on the far side of the camp. They are yelling and laughing, when one of them suddenly stops, frozen. A look of horror forms on his face and he points directly behind you. The other children sense something is wrong and stop to look.

You turn to see what he is pointing at.

Go on to the next page.

You are less then twenty feet from a giant sloth. It looks like an enormous badger, with arms as long as its legs, and a small mean-looking face. The sloth stands up on its hind legs and emits a bellow. The children scamper into the tundra. Grandmother runs to grab a spear, and the sloth makes a move after her. You have to do something!

You frantically search for a weapon. The only thing you see is the long wooden fire stirrer. You swoop down and grab the thick burning branch. Instinctively you swing it once all the way around, and throw it like a shot put at the sloth's snarling face.

Turn to the next page.

Yes! The branch throws off a shower of sparks and the sharp burning end hits the sloth in the face. He yelps in surprise, blinded. A coal clings to the matted fur near his eye. He yells in pain as he swipes blindly at the hot burning coal. Grandmother thrusts the spear into the sloth's side. It goes in a foot. The sloth roars with pain and anger, falling onto the spear. The spear now goes completely through its side, killing it, thanks to the sharp flint point.

When the mammoth hunters return empty-handed that evening, a feast of roasted sloth meat welcomes them. Thanks are given to the Great Spirit and to the Fire. Grandmother gives you the new rabbit skin blanket the next day as her personal thanks.

"You saved my life," she says simply.

"But you killed the sloth," you answer humbly, accepting the valuable gift.

The story of the day you killed the sloth becomes legend in your tribe's oral history and is retold for over a thousand years.

The End

You grab a spear from the remaining pile near the edge of camp and run to catch up with the others.

You learn that the boy who found you after coming through the wormhole is named Errkun.

The mood among the group is lighthearted for the first hour but becomes more serious as you approach the hunting grounds. One of the leaders, a thin young man around fifteen, signals everyone to stop.

"Asketh, our scout, spotted the herd of young mammoth about two fets from here, near the Great Ice," he begins. He draws with a stick in the dirt. "The narrow route through the Ice to the long valley is here," he adds. Several among the group nod in comprehension.

"How shall we hunt today?" a woman asks.

"We can steer them into the narrow path and topple a boulder," suggests an older man.

"I thought Asketh said that one of the mammoths looked weak," another woman adds. "One of its tusks is broken."

"The fast ones could circle and approach from the opposite way," Errkun suggests. "The herd would scatter and the weak one would be last to move."

Go on to the next page.

You are both frightened and excited. You suddenly notice everyone glancing in your direction. Why?

Finally the oldest man asks, "Would you mind if we used the route to the long valley, since the last time we did so, your father was killed there?"

You need to make a decision.

If you say that you think the group will have more luck by scattering the herd and going after the weak mammoth, turn to the next page.

If you say that it is okay to use the route to the long valley, that a kill there would honor your father's memory, turn to page 33.

While you feel reluctant to prey upon a weakened animal, you know it is the key to survival for your tribe. Even a small mammoth will feed all thirty-six of you for more than a month.

"I think we should chase the mammoths in the open," you reply, "and avoid the area near the glacier."

Everyone nods and no one argues. The young hunt leader designates a split into two groups a short distance later. You are part of the team to descend into the flat plains to circle back around from the scrub forest on the other side. Your job will be to scare the mammoth herd into the trap of the others, waiting to spear them from below. The trip takes almost two hours, and the sun is past the high point in the sky when you finally creep up and peer over a ridge at the herd below.

The man named Asketh, who was also the scout, pulls something carefully from a string around his waist. It is a small animal horn, from an oryx, you think. He blows the horn; it makes a funny high-pitched sound. The entire mammoth herd looks toward the ridge. The largest mammoth grunts several times, and trumpets. At this signal, the mammoths turn to run in the opposite direction. Your group runs quickly over the ridge after them, waving their arms and yelling. Several people blow horns.

Turn to page 32.

The mammoths continue to run. Sure enough, one is straggling far behind. It is missing part of its left tusk. You are less than fifty feet away, when it stops. It turns and charges directly at you and Errkun.

Without thinking, you position your spear to throw, and wait. When the beast is less than ten feet away, towering over you, you aim and throw as hard as you can. Errkun alongside of you does the same.

Your spear pierces the thick wooly hide of the animal just at the shoulder. It barely makes a dent. But Errkun's spear hits the bull's-eye, driving deep into the animal's mouth. You both jump aside just before being trampled. The mammoth runs another twenty feet before staggering to a halt, dropping to its knees and rolling over.

Now your people will eat well. It is a good-sized mammoth and will provide dried meat for many months this winter. That night you say a prayer of thanks to the Great Spirit for keeping your people alive for another year.

The End

"It would honor my father's memory to make a kill where he was killed," you say. "Let us steer the herd toward the route to the Long Valley."

Everyone nods and you notice several people rub their foreheads twice quickly with their thumb. You are not sure if it's a prayer for your father or a wish for good luck in the hunt.

The young man leading splits the group into two. You are directed to be with Errkun and four others, and you are assigned to the entrance through the Great Ice.

As Errkun comes into step alongside you, he whispers, "I know exactly which boulder we should seek to kill the mammoth."

You arrive at the break in the Great Ice around thirty minutes later. It is as wide as two mammoths side by side.

"There," Erkun, points to a spot with some rocks emerging from the ice about 400 feet up the side of the glacier. He scrambles ahead and you follow. It is colder here and the path is slippery. You get into position behind the boulder. It indeed is perfectly placed for toppling into the narrow path below.

The group has split into three. Two more boulder perches are manned on the other side of the gap. Everyone sets in for the wait.

Turn to page 35.

You know that this is a brutal way to kill the majestic mammoth, but it means survival for you and your people. You must get meat for winter. The smaller animals are getting scarce. And the season for hunting will be over soon.

You must have fallen asleep, for the next thing you know, Errkun is shaking you awake. "They are coming," he whispers.

You peer around the boulder and see six woolly mammoths, each as tall as a house, thundering toward the narrow path. You look across the gorge, and see the two other outposts, ready to push the boulders. Errkun watches carefully, and then commands, "Now."

The two of you push but nothing happens.

You grab your spear, and use it as a lever. Errkun watches you, stunned.

The boulder tumbles down the side of the glacier, and hits the first mammoth in the rear hip. The beast trumpets in pain, but continues on.

"Watch out!" Erkun yells.

You look back to see a small avalanche of rocks and dislodged ice hurtle down.

Turn to the next page.

Suddenly you lose your footing. You fall onto the ice and begin sliding down the side of the glacier, into the path of the oncoming mammoths. They trumpet, angry now, and stampede toward you.

You see your life at home in New Mexico flash before your eyes. You see your parents, your favorite horse, the ranch, your collection of ancient pottery shards. You frantically look around for a way out. As you do, you notice a small rock carved with a spiral. You reach out toward it. Everything goes dark as the first mammoth hoof comes down on your chest.

Go on to the next page.

You jerk awake, yelling. You are lying on the grass in the small garden behind Grandpa Jasper's study. Your father sticks his head out the window and asks, "What are you yelling about? It's dinnertime."

The End

You reach out and brush your fingers gently over the ancient symbol of the flute player. Your eyes are bathed in white light even as you close them. You try to walk but you feel no gravity. You realize you are floating. Very slowly, the scenery around you emerges. A girl with copper-colored skin and long black braids stands over you, blocking the sun. She is wearing a loose simple dress of rough cotton that is a faded pink color. Leather moccasins covered in a pattern of geometric black and white cover her feet. You notice that they tie at the ankle.

"Sleeping again?" she demands. "We are supposed to be picking berries for the feast. You are so lazy! Come on!"

You want to defend yourself, but you are too shocked to say anything. You scramble up and brush the sand from your clothes. They are also made of cotton and are a light green. You are staring at a beautiful valley facing east, with high cliffs to the north and south. Huge ponderosa pine trees grow near the stream running along the valley floor. A hawk circles lazily overhead. You run to catch up to the girl with braids who is heading west up the canyon.

"When is the feast?" you ask.

The girl rolls her eyes.

Turn to the next page.

"It's the harvest feast. Tonight. Just because you are a talented carver does not mean that you don't have to help. Everyone in the tribe is working on the feast as we speak. Hundreds of people. We have lots of berries to pick."

You scurry to keep up. A short time later you come to a patch of wild blackberry bushes and begin. The sun is hot overhead, and your arms and shoulders soon ache. But in a few hours you and the girl have picked two large baskets of beautiful berries.

Go on to the next page.

"Bandelier!" you exclaim out loud.

"What?" the girl asks, irritated.

You turn red in embarrassment. You have suddenly realized where you are. You came here once with your grandfather, although that was seven hundred years in the future. You are in Bandelier National Park, near Los Alamos, but it's seven hundred years in the past. The baskets are what reminded you. They are from the Tewa, the ancient people also called the Anasazi. Your grandfather once pointed out the baskets at the museum in Santa Fe. You have gone back in time to the era of the Anasazi, precursors to today's modern Pueblo Indians. The Anasazi peoples and their advanced civilization in the high mesas and river valleys of New Mexico have always fascinated you. These gentle farming people had developed permanent communities with rituals and laws, as well as ceremonies that were complex and wonderful.

Wonderful except for maybe the short-tempered girl who thinks she has to boss you around.

"Now what?" you ask.

"We deliver the berries to the cook lodge, and get dressed for the feast," she says, sighing at your stupidity.

You gasp as you come into sight of the famous Bandelier longhouse, home to more than 100 families.

Turn to the next page.

The longhouse is even more impressive than you imagined. But you need to keep pace as you follow your berry-picking partner back to the cook lodge. Several women look up as you arrive. One of them approaches.

"You're late," the woman says, reaching for the baskets. "And you're in trouble" she adds, looking at you. "The elders have asked that you go to the kiva immediately."

The girl with braids is about to complain, but this news stops even her.

"The kiva?" you ask. "Are you sure?

Kivas are the most sacred places in the whole pueblo. It is where all the most important rituals and ceremonies are performed. Why would they want to see you there? It must be a grave violation of the Medicine Wheel, to demand your presence in the middle of feast preparations.

"Okay, I will go," you reply. You noticed the kivas to the south as you approached the longhouse. Several women who are cooking look furtively in your direction.

Go on to the next page.

You walk back along the path in the direction of the kiva. A young boy approaches.

"You are in big trouble! They found a mask of one of the sacred kachinas under your bed in the longhouse. What were you thinking, stealing it? I would be careful if I were you," he whispers.

"But I didn't steal anything," you protest, as the boy hurries on.

The elders think you stole a kachina mask? This is serious! The kachinas are intermediaries to the gods. It is against the ways of your people to pray directly to the Great Spirit. Instead you pray to the kachinas, and the kachinas go to the gods for help. They send prayers for enough sun and rain, for the corn, the squash, and the beans. They help protect the place where you live from hostile warrior bands, like the Apache to the south.

You look all around. You notice the ladders and handholds on the cliffs to the north that go all the way to the top. Should you escape? Or should you go and defend yourself? This could be punishable by banishment, which could mean death.

If you decide to climb the cliffs to escape, turn to the next page.

If you decide to go to the kiva and find out what has happened, turn to page 51.

You scan the cliffs, trying to determine the best route up. There is no time to waste. You know it by instinct. You need to get out, now!

You are suddenly startled by the scream of a hawk that circles above you. It dives and swoops. Its white tail feathers sparkle in the sun. Is this hawk a symbol sent to guide you? You have to think like an Anasazi if you are going to escape. Maybe it is a shaman who has changed from human form into a bird? You watch where the bird goes. It seems to be directing you to a route to the top. You look around. In the other direction, you spot a path that heads north.

If you decide to follow the bird, turn to page 46.

If you decide it's safer to ignore the hawk and take the path, turn to page 79.

46

You leave the well-worn footpath and scramble up the hill to the base of the cliff. The soil is sandy and loose and the climbing is tough. You are out of breath before you have started. You hear someone yell below, and you turn to look. It is a young man, maybe twenty years old, who has emerged from the kiva. He is running and pointing at you. You decide to climb a ladder to one of the many storage caves dug by hand in the soft red sandstone.

You look down as the young man from the kiva reaches the base of the cliff and begins to climb.

Get moving! you say to yourself.

The toeholds are small, old, and not very deep. Up you go, one by one, hoping you will not fall.

The first hundred yards up are in full sight of the people below, but no one else is following. You hear the young man curse as he slips. But there is not time to look. Finally you make it to the crack in the cliff face where you cannot be seen from below. You are almost safe!

Turn to page 48.

48

You reach the top of the cliff and look all around. You are standing on the mesa. You can see for miles. Bandelier lies below you. It is a perfect box canyon with a narrow opening at both ends. This makes it easy to defend. You scan the surrounding area but see no one. Where, you wonder, are the lookouts who are supposed to warn the tribe if enemies approach?

If the Anasazi below want to capture you, they could send a party up to the mesa via another route. Perhaps they have already signaled someone on lookout, and that is why you see no one. He might be hiding in ambush.

It's time to head away from the pueblo below. But in what direction? You have no food, no water, and no supplies of any sort. How will you survive and where will you go?

Just then you spy the hawk circling overhead.

Go on to the next page.

The hawk is silent, but it swings small arcs around you. Then it flies off to the north. It returns and once again flies north. Is this your spirit animal? Is she leading you to safety?

North will lead to the mountains and the forests of giant pines. There will be water. But how long will it take? Are there hostile people about? You must start moving.

The first steps are the hardest. Then you get into a rhythm and move quickly over the mesa. Piñon and juniper dot the dry earth. Beware of snakes, you remind yourself. In a few hours, you reach a wide path—almost thirty feet across. It looks like a road. You remember reading that some anthropologists thought these paths had religious significance or astronomical meaning. Some said they were oriented to the summer solstice. Others said they were trade routes. The road travels along an east-west axis.

If you take the road west, toward the mountains and the setting sun, go on to the next page.

If you take the road east, where the mesa slopes down to the valley several thousand feet below, turn to page 74.

50

You point yourself west and walk toward the sun as it sets. Your eyes suddenly catch movement to the south. It is a blur of tawny brownish gold. It's a mountain lion! These predators hunt deer and elk, but humans taste just fine to them as well. They share this territory with bears. You don't want to meet either. Again you see the blur of movement. You freeze. What should you do?

If you stand completely still, hoping the mountain lion will pass on by and leave you alone, turn to page 59.

If you make a run for it, turn to page 62.

You know you did not steal the kachina mask. So who put the mask under your bed? You decide to go to the kiva and defend yourself to the elders. It's a risk, but the chances of escaping Bandelier are also slim.

You mount the sloping roof of the kiva. There is a round hole at the top in the center, about the size of a broad-shouldered man. A ladder projects just over the lip of the entrance hole.

You hesitate. Is it fear or a premonition? You are aware of the sudden envelope of silence around you. Where is the noise of a large community going about its tasks, preparing for the harvest feast? Is the kiva that powerful?

You raise your right leg and place your foot on the first rung of the ladder right below the opening.

Turn to the next page.

So far, so good. You put your other foot on the rung and descend into the darkness. It is like entering a world of velvet, smooth and all embracing. There is a smell of incense, probably from a mix of piñon and juniper.

Three more rungs. One more. Then a voice.

"Leave fear behind you. Embrace the Great Spirit."

Peering into the darkness, your eyes begin to adjust to the light inside. Three men, old, seated around a sand painting that you can just make out, await you.

"Come. I can see that you have left fear behind. It is never a friend."

Turn to page 55.

You have always been fascinated by the kachinas. This is an extraordinary chance. You know in your heart how proud Grandpa Jasper would be with your decision.

"I am honored by your request," you say, bowing your head slightly to the elders.

They nod. One of the elders stands and draws a symbol in the sand next to the hearth.

A chill runs down your spine. It's the spiral symbol, the one you saw on the kiva wall back at the ranch.

"And when you need to travel between worlds, just come here and draw this in the sand," the old man says. "And do this."

He erases the spiral with his moccasin, and disappears in a puff of smoke.

The End

A calmness comes over you. This was the right decision. You are sure of it.

Two more figures climb down the ladder. They are younger. One of them smiles at you. You recognize him as a rock artist. He is eager to learn some of your skills in woodcarving and also learn about the symbols that you carve into the masks.

"You have been chosen to become a carver for our tribe. We believe that you have the gift. It is one of the most important of the sacred tasks. Will you accept our teaching and direction?"

The voice is that of the oldest man, who is seated cross-legged in front of a small fire that smolders in a pit next to the sand painting.

"I thought that you were going to accuse me of stealing the kachina mask they found in my room," you reply. "They told me to come to the kiva."

The old man smiles. "That was just a test of your bravery," he answers. "By coming here you have shown you have courage."

You must make a decision. You have always been fascinated by the symbols of the kachinas. But you sense that if you accept this position, you might never be able to return to the present time. What should you do?

If you accept their request to train as a sacred carver of kachinas, turn to page 53.

If you say you cannot accept, turn to page 69.

You reach for the small log raft depicting a person fishing with a spear. Cold and shivers instantly overcome you. And you feel wet!

Your eyes are closed and when you open them, you are flailing around in the ocean. You lick your lips and taste salt. And the water is cold!

"Help!" you cry. "Help me!"

You look around and see the shore, but it's at least a quarter mile away. The currents are strong and you guess the water temperature is below 50 degrees. You won't last for long at this temperature. You guess that you have five or six minutes before hypothermia sets in. If your core temperature drops below 86 degrees, it will never go back up to 98, and you will die. The sea is not kind.

Turn to the next page.

58

"Help!" you yell again.

You hear voices and whirl around. A small crude dugout canoe approaches. A man wearing a sealskin anorak garment stands in the bow, holding a spear. Is he going to aim it at you?

Instead he pushes it toward you and motions you to grab hold. As he pulls you in, he reaches out, grabs your hand, and pulls you aboard.

You lie in the roughly made log canoe like a landed fish. The man covers you with an animal skin. Your teeth chatter and your muscles shake. You need more than animal skin to warm you. Has hypothermia already started?

No. The fisherman poles to shore, where a small group of huts surround a fire. That should warm you. You are hauled to the fire by several of the fishermen, and covered with more skins. They give you a bitter-tasting hot fluid and motion you to drink it all. The people, including women, who leave the huts gather around. They point at your clothes and hair. But they seem friendly enough.

The man who saved you is conferring with a much taller, broad-shouldered older man. He wears a wolf-skin headdress complete with eyeholes, ears, nose, and teeth. He must be the headman of the tribe.

Turn to page 61.

You stand as still as you can and extend your arms to look as large and as menacing as possible. You can hear your heart beating. The dry warm wind blows around you.

You wait. And wait. And wait.

You no longer see the tawny blur of the mountain lion. Is he gone? Does he seek other prey? Thirty minutes must have passed.

Carefully you lower your arms, and scan the surrounding area. All clear. You take a step, then another. It's still all clear. Now you begin walking again, slowly but steadily.

As night falls, you spot a light in the distance. You approach cautiously.

Turn to the next page.

You carefully peer around a boulder. It is a hunting party from the tribe that lives on the other side of the mountains. They are friends and greet you and give you water and food. One of them asks you to look at an unusual symbol on a rock he found earlier that day. He mentions your well-known skill at carving.

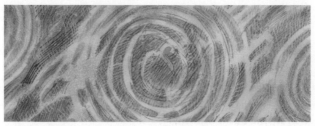

"I don't know what this symbol means," he says handing you a small river stone. You accept the stone and everything goes white in front your eyes. The floating sensation returns. As your sight slowly comes back, you are standing in the kiva back at your grandfather's ranch. You can tell by the color of the sky overhead that only a minute or two has passed since you left. You look at the stone in your hand. It's the spiral symbol. It matches the spirals carved on the kiva petroglyph in front of you. This must be what your grandfather meant when he said, "If you pay close attention, it will lead you home." The spiral symbol signifies return.

And return home for dinner is what you need to do right this minute!

The End

You try to sit, but the tea has made you lightheaded. Maybe it was a drug or even a poison. You are beginning to have visions of huge rainbows and roaring forest fires. You don't like this feeling one bit. You have lost control of your ability to think clearly. This is dangerous.

The wolf-head leader approaches you. You notice his piercing eyes. He is not smiling. Then he speaks.

"Strange one, where are you from? You are not one of us. Are you our enemy or our friend?"

If you choose to tell them the truth about time travel and who you are, turn to page 63.

If you pretend to be lost and are a friend and not a foe, turn to page 65.

62

You decide to run for it. Big mistake!!! Your running attracts the big cat. It sprints toward you. The powerful muscles in his shoulders and legs drive him forward at enormous speed.

A few seconds later, he reaches you.

You are lost, his prey and his reward.

The End

Perhaps the tea has affected your judgment. On the other hand, you have always been very honest. You blurt out your story of living thousands of years in the future.

"I come from the age of computers, and the Internet. We have had plane flight for over 100 years. Many people have cars to get around instead of horses or boats," you say.

You decide to leave out the parts about gunpowder and flying saucers.

At first the people listen, fascinated. But then something shifts. Fear crosses their faces. They turn to their leader, the man with the wolf headdress. Something doesn't feel right.

Again he asks who you are. You repeat your story, adding more details about the kiva and your grandfather.

The tribal elder beckons several men to the side. They confer for several minutes, looking at you and pointing. A decision is made.

Turn to the next page.

64

Two young men in the tribe approach and grab you roughly. They lead you to the shore near their camp and put you into one of the small log rafts waiting there. Then they push you out into the rough sea. All they have given you is a single sealskin to wrap yourself against the bitter wind.

The currents pick up the boat, and carry you south. You try to figure out where you are. It looks like the Oregon coast. Within minutes you can barely see the people waiting and watching from the shore.

They have cast you out. From the state of their small clay and wood huts, and their skill with fire, you guess they are 6,000 years in the past. That means they are still in Paleo-Indian times. And this means they are in sheer survival mode. You pose a possible danger to their survival. You represent the unknown. The truth of your story frightened them.

What will happen to you now?

The End

You pause to think carefully about what to say. You need to convince these people that you are friend and not foe. These wandering Paleo-Indian bands of between 20 and 60 people are always in sheer survival mode. Any major mistake could mean the end of their people. Friendship between bands or groups is not common but not unheard of either.

They all stare at you, awaiting your answer. You know from your studies that their language is not complex. It is simple and direct.

"Well," you begin, "I am..."

The people move ever so slightly toward you. Is it hostile?

"I was with another group. But we were caught in a storm. Our raft broke apart. Three others perished at sea."

You realize that the word "perish" is not in their vocabulary.

"Three of our party died. They drowned," you explain further.

Turn to the next page.

The headman nods and turns to the two men beside him. They talk in low tones for several minutes. It feels like hours to you.

Is your fate being decided right now?

"Look, I am a good fisherman. I know how to use nets, fishing spears. I know how to dry the fish. I can be a help to the tribe."

The headman with the wolf-skin hat seems to listen. The others are waiting for him to make the decision. You know that justice—if that is what you can call it—is swift and complete. Survival of his people is all about making the right choices. If you are seen as an enemy, they might believe that there are others with you, hiding and ready to attack at your signal.

Suddenly you get an idea, and feel in your pocket. It's there!

Go on to the next page.

Your cell phone made it through the wormhole in time. Should you take their picture? Or would that scare them too much?

If you decide to pull out the cell phone and take some pictures, turn to the next page.

If you decide to hang tight and await the headman's decision, turn to page 72.

What the heck? You are probably about to get kicked out of the camp anyway. It can't hurt to try your cell phone.

You pull it from your back pocket. Luckily your parents had given you a waterproof cover for it.

You turn it on and hold it in the direction of two small girls playing. Snap! You take their photo. Everyone has stopped talking and stares at you.

You hold up the smart phone.

"Look!" you exclaim. "Photo!"

Everyone crowds forward to take a look.

Turn to page 70.

"I'm afraid I cannot do this for you," you say. There is a tremor in your voice. "I am...very sorry."

"Are you sure?" the elders ask in unison.

You nod yes.

You climb back out of the kiva with a heavy heart. That night you participate in the harvest feast. It is a joyous event that lasts until dawn. You eat and dance and sing. No one mentions the kachina mask, or your decision, during the feast or afterward.

It turns out that you have a talent for plants. You become one of the best farmers of the tribe. Years pass, and you watch and wait for some sign for a way to return to the present.

You still have not found it.

The End

70

The people are amazed at what they see. You quickly take another picture. This time you capture the adults that have surrounded you. They gasp in surprise and laugh.

The headman makes an announcement.

"You are a god!" he cries. He gets on one knee and bows his head. "This is magic."

Everyone wants his or her picture taken. The old ones cannot stop laughing. A little boy runs up and gives you a kiss on the cheek. You have gone from threat to the most popular god in the universe.

That night the people cook a special feast. They make you eat until you cannot take another bite. You know that this is the highest form of honor they can bestow, in a world where survival is still a daily challenge.

The next morning, you awaken in a warm hut, covered in animal skins. The elder women knock and bring you a set of sealskin clothes that fit perfectly.

It is good to be a god for that day and the next. Until the smart phone's battery finally gives out. The headman lets you stay. But you are given the lowest job in the village, digging the latrines.

The End

You decide it's best to leave your cell phone where it is. You can use it later if there is a good opportunity and purpose.

"Please, I want to help!" you simply add.

Slowly the headman approaches. His eyes once again search yours. He looks at your head and your hair. Then he grabs your hands, turning them over and examining them. He shakes his head. You realize that your hands are smooth and not calloused. They are not the hands of a worker, or a fisherman.

Your clothes are also strange to him. You are still wearing jeans and a blue T-shirt. Your shoes are gone. Compared to the tribe members, you are taller and leaner. The headman continues to study you. You sense the others getting nervous.

Go on to the next page.

Finally, the headman turns to the others and announces, "I can see that this being is godlike. This being does not labor and yet has great health and vigor. I believe this might be a god, from another world. I sense the power and goodness here." He turns to you and bows deeply. "We welcome you to our band."

The rest of the tribe drops to their knees and bows their heads in your direction.

Wow! You have just escaped a potentially deadly end. Good for you. Now, how to get home?

Or maybe you should stick around and observe them? You might learn a lot and your career as an anthropologist back in present time would be made!

The End

You decide to take the wide path toward the east. As with most long journeys, the first steps are the hardest. But soon you have a rhythm.

An hour later, the path begins to descend. You are halfway to the valley floor when it becomes too dark to continue. You spot a small rock overhang. It makes a good shelter to spend the night.

You sleep fitfully. But morning comes and you feel awake and alive. You find some old pine cones on the ground. They become your breakfast.

You are thirsty but the first water is probably not for another half-day's walk. And that's if you're lucky. It's still early and the air is cool. Now is the time to make tracks.

Go on to the next page.

You walk as quickly as you dare. If you become overheated and sweat, it will only make you thirstier. You are nearing the valley floor, when you see some dark green sage off to the left. Usually, this color means water nearby.

If you head in the direction of the dark green sage, turn to the next page.

If you continue straight ahead where you know you will eventually reach the Rio Grande, turn to page 77.

76

You decide to walk in the direction of the dark green sage. It takes you over an hour to get there. But when you do, there is no water to be found. There are some dark red berries, however. You have never seen them before. But at least they would provide some moisture. They could also be poisonous.

If you decide to return to your original path toward the Rio Grande, go on to the next page.

If you decide to eat some berries, turn to page 78.

You decide to continue to the valley floor. Eventually you will reach the Rio Grande. You walk for another hour. When the sun is high overhead, you sit under a juniper bush to wait out the heat of the day. At sundown you get up. You are so thirsty, you are dizzy. But you have no choice but to continue.

The Medicine Wheel must be protecting you. The next thing you know, you see a muddy pond up ahead. You dive into it face-first. Even though the water is brackish, you have never tasted anything so delicious. It is enough to get you through the rest of the day. When you reach the Rio Grande that night, you must crawl the last 100 feet.

You spend the next two days recovering from your journey. You drink water in small amounts until you are re-hydrated. You decide to continue along the river valley. No one is more surprised than you when you turn a bend in the river two days later and come across three men fishing next to an SUV.

You have walked through the Trail of Lost Time.

The End

The berries are just too tempting to pass up. Your mouth is so dry. Death would be welcome, you think.

You eat several handfuls. They are mildly sweet, which is a good sign. Soon however you grow drowsy and slump to the desert floor. You are awakened by terrible stomach cramps.

"There, there, sweetheart," you mother suddenly says. "It's just a bad dream. Here, have some warm milk. This should put you back to sleep."

You sip the liquid thirstily. Was the kiva a dream? You look at your bedside table and see your grandfather's letter covered in red dust.

Hmmmmm.

The End

You ignore the cries of the disappearing hawk heading west. Instead you follow the faint path heading north. It snakes along the edge of the mesa. You think you pass what is modern day Los Alamos. It's nothing but some gently rolling hills at the edge of a pinon forest. The line of the mountaintops behind it is what gives the location away. It may be a thriving town of 100,000 people, but today there's neither a soul or a house to be seen. As you stare at the horizon, you become aware of the sound of pounding hooves.

Is it the elders coming after you?

You scan the area, frantic to find a hiding place. You spot an arroyo nearby. Maybe you can hide there while the horse and rider passes? You really have no choice. The sound of the horse's hooves is getting louder. You make a run for it and leap over the edge of the arroyo.

Turn to page 80.

80

The arroyo, a dry gully created by runoffs from quick summer rainstorms, is about eight feet deep. You roll as you land, to soften the blow. Even so, you manage to give your shoulder a good scrape. You lie there quietly, listening, making yourself small against the earth. Sure enough the horse and rider approach and then ride past. You wait until you can't hear them any more, and scramble to your feet. You are dusting off your fringed, beaded leggings when you hear it. Your heart practically stops.

"Chh..chh..chh..chh..chh..chh..chh.."

You stay stock still and quickly scan the red sandy floor with your eyes.

A RATTLESNAKE!

Turn to page 82.

The bite of a rattlesnake is a horrible and almost certain death. Its powerful venom can cause total body paralysis–while you bleed to death internally.

Unfortunately, that is the only detail you remember from your science unit on rattlesnakes. You now wish that you had paid attention about what to do if you ran into one. Like right now.

You try to think. Did Miss Muff say that the rattle means the snake is about to bite? Should you make a run for it? Or are you supposed to stay as still as a statue?

If you decide to stay as still as a statue, go on to the next page.

If you decide to run for your life in the opposite direction, turn to page 88.

You decide to stay still and hope the snake understands that you don't mean any harm.

Unfortunately, the rattling continues. What's worse, the rattlesnake slowly uncoils and slithers forward.

"Please! I mean you no harm!" you cry, as if the rattlesnake speaks English. You close your eyes tight.

"I know that," a voice says. "I wanted to give you a warning."

You open your eyes and look to see where the voice came from. But you are alone in the arroyo. There is no one else around.

"It is time to go home," the voice continues. "A war party is approaching from the north."

You whip your head around, looking for someone. But the arroyo is completely empty.

"A war party?" you ask, hoping you can figure out where the voice is coming from.

Turn to the next page.

"Yes, a war party," the voice answers.

You stare at the snake. It's mouth just moved.

"Did you just speak?" you ask.

"Yes," the snake answers. "I did. How good of you to notice. Now I repeat, a war party is coming. It's time to go home."

"But…that's not so easy," you say.

You cannot believe you are speaking to a snake! Is this a strange dream? You feel a stab of pain from the scrape on your shoulder and decide not.

"I know, I know," the snake says. "You came through the magic petroglyph. The one on your grandfather's ranch, far into the future."

"What?!" you cry. "How can you know that?"

"I am one of the Snake People. I take this form to see things. I am here today to warn you. It is time to go," he answers.

"I would love to go. But how?" you exclaim.

"Take this," the snake replies.

He slithers to where you stand, and shakes his rattler furiously. The tip suddenly breaks off. It flies through the air and hits you in the leg.

"Take that in your hand and think of home," the snake advises. "Quickly. They are coming."

You notice the sound of pounding hooves. But it's way more than one horse. This time it sounds like hundreds!

Turn to page 86.

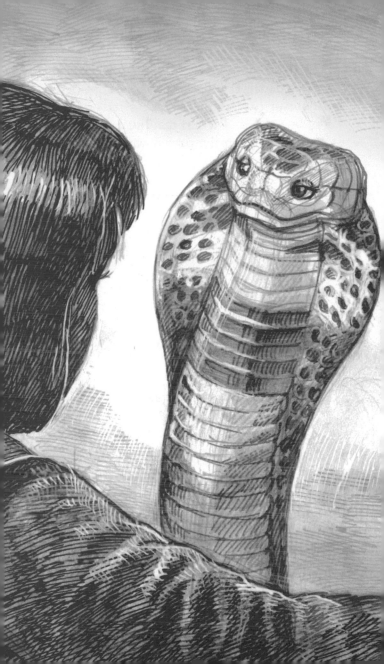

86

"That's all? Just hold the rattle?" you ask, looking down. But the snake has disappeared. You bend over to grab the tip of his rattle and grasp it in your hand. The last thing you see is a young warrior riding up the arroyo with a spear, ready to kill you.

Go on to the next page.

You open your eyes and look around. You're home in bed, in the guest room at your grandpa Jasper's ranch.

"Was that a dream?" you say out loud to no one in particular.

You can smell bacon cooking in the kitchen. The sun is out. Your cat Leroy is at the foot of your bed. He stretches out and meows. You reach forward to give him a snug when a small brown object falls out of your hand and on to the floor.

You look down. It's the tip of a rattlesnake's tail. Maybe that's what they mean by shake, rattle, and roll?

The End

88

You decide to run from the rattler in the opposite direction. Whatever the rattle means, it can't be a good sign. You take a couple of deep breaths to oxygenate your blood.

"One...two...three..." you count silently. "Go!"

You hurl your legs as fast as they will go, running away from the rattlesnake. The arroyo narrows quickly. You are going to have to scramble out soon, you think. You have no idea if the snake is coming after you. You don't have the nerve to look back.

Go on to the next page.

The arroyo bends and you round the corner...
Smack! Right into the entrance to a cave.

You once read about how snakes like to winter over in caves. But it's summer. So you should be okay. You slow to a walk as you enter the darkness. This might be a good place to hole up until the elders stop looking for you.

You pause to let your eyes get used to the light and to catch your breath. Gradually you can make out large shapes of boulders. In the far end of the cave, you spot a faint source of light. What is it? You walk forward. The floor of the cave is smooth and sandy. It almost looks like a path. But a path to where?

Turn to the next page.

You follow the sandy path toward the faint light to the rear of the cave.

As you move forward, the light gets brighter. It must be a way out, you think, putting another foot forward. But instead of a sandy path, there is…nothing!

You topple forward and feel the air rushing past as you fall hundreds of feet. You feel almost weightless as you continue to drop. Shouldn't you have hit the bottom by now? It almost feels like you are slowing down and floating. Is this heaven?

Go on to the next page.

THUNK!

You hit the ground and sit up. Then you shake your head to clear it, and look around.

There are two tunnels leading away from where you sit. One has a flaming torch sitting in a fancy golden bracket. The other tunnel is dark, except for some daylight reflected on a wall in the distance.

If you enter the other tunnel with daylight in the distance, turn to page 92.

If you decide to take the flaming torch and explore that tunnel, turn to page 107.

92

You decide to feel your way carefully down the dark tunnel toward the daylight. Sure enough, when you turn the corner, there is light coming from a hole in the far wall. The tunnel narrows and shortens. You need to get down on all fours to reach the opening. You pull yourself through and fall end over end. You are someplace on a steep dry slope covered in a strange, stiff grass. Phew! You stare into the bright sun overhead. It's the same sun, at least.

You get up off the ground and brush the dust off of your leggings. You scan the terrain around you. It's the desert, but it doesn't look like New Mexico. A wide, flat valley stretches out in front of you. You peer into it and gasp.

Go on to the next page.

"The Nazca lines! Is this Peru?" you say out loud.

The flat valley floor is covered in dozens of enormous geoglyphs, or carvings. The images are hundreds of feet across. You can make out a hummingbird, a giant lizard, and the famous Nazca monkey with the spiral tail. Grandpa Jasper used to talk about the Nazca lines all the time.

"How did a people in 400 ad create images that could only be seen from the sky?" he used to ask. "And the more important question is why."

The Nazca lines are one of the great mysteries of archeology.

In the distance you see people working. They are in the middle of carving a new line, but it's not an animal figure. It's a geometric shape. The people are digging the red pebble surface to reveal the white hard-pack underneath. Should you go ask them who they are and what they are doing? You are hungry, tired, and thirsty. Is it safe to approach? There appear to be other people posted on watch. They are carrying bows with arrows and stand apart from the rest.

If you decide to approach the people working on the desert floor, turn to page 94.

If you decide to steer clear of the people carving in the earth and try to find some water and food first, turn to page 99.

You scramble down the hillside switchback style. It's too steep for a direct route. When you reach the desert floor, the people are farther away that they looked from above. You march toward them, your eyes alert. As you get closer, you can hear them talking and laughing. They don't sound like slaves. One of the guards let's out a whoop. He says something rapidly to the group. Everyone turns to look in your direction. There is no one and nothing visible for miles. Except you.

You try to walk confidently, but you are starting to feel a tiny bit nervous. The workers are talking animatedly among themselves and pointing. One of the women throws down her digging tool and shouts something to the others. She begins to run toward you. Everyone else quickly joins her.

If you decide to stand your ground, turn to page 96.

If you decide to turn around and run, turn to page 102.

The carvers give you some water and a type of corn cake filled with vegetables. It's the first food you have had since lunch, yesterday or whenever it was. It tastes delicious.

They try to carry you, but you insist on walking, as the whole group leads you back to a settlement at the edge of the desert. A hush comes over the village when you enter. Everyone in the small cluster of stone buildings stops and kneels as you pass by. You expect to meet the village headman, but instead they lead you to what turns out to be some sort of clinic. There are six people inside, including a small girl, and they are all very sick.

"You may heal our friends, now," the guard says. "We will leave you to work alone." With that he disappears back outside.

"Heal?" you start to say. But he is gone.

I am not a healer, you think. What can you do? You look around at the people lying on small cots. They look sick, but no one appears to be on the verge of death. You may not be a healer, but you know a couple of things about staying healthy. You pretend to be one of your parents and start by asking questions.

"Is it a sore throat? An earache? Do you have a fever? When did it start? Do you feel sick to your stomach?"

Turn to page 98.

96

You decide to stand your ground. In truth, there's not much of anywhere to run.

It's a strange sight, thirty people running toward you, yelling and whooping. They are dressed in colorful cotton tunics, and wide straw hats. Some of them are flapping their arms, like birds.

As they get closer, they begin to slow down. Your heart beats wildly in your chest. You raise your empty hands to show that you carry no weapons and come in peace. This has a very strange effect.

The workers come to a sudden halt, less then fifty feet away. No one says anything. Some of they look awestruck. Then they all drop to their knees. The guards approach and kneel and bow. One of them raises his head to speak. Although it is a strange, guttural language that you have never heard in your life, you can understand what he says.

"Oh Great One! We have waited long for you. We welcome your return to Earth. These carvings are but a small offering of thanks for all you have done for our people."

Return to Earth? Do these people think you're some kind of Martian?

Turn to page 95.

It does not take long to learn that everyone in the clinic had been traveling together the week before when they fell ill. You ask a few more questions, and realize that they all drank from the same small well.

"Did everyone who drank from the well become ill?" you ask.

They shake their heads yes.

You nod, trying to look wise.

"I have the prescription," you announce.

They all look up. You point at a small jug on a table.

"You must all drink two of these per day, but you must boil the water for thirty minutes beforehand," you announce. "Do this for one week and you will be well."

The Nazca are good patients and so exactly as you say. In a week they are all well. Even the old shaman befriends you.

You know now that when you return to your own place and time, you want to be a doctor and heal people everywhere.

The End

You skitter across the steep hill, and down, away from the people carving in the earth. The land is flat and barren. How will you find food and water here? There aren't even any cacti. You walk for an hour, hugging the foot of the hill. But even the hill disappears eventually, joining the great flat desert plain. You stand for a moment to gather your thoughts. The sun burns hot overhead. All of a sudden you wish you were back home and had never taken this journey. You almost miss the rattlesnake.

Suddenly you trip over the edge of one of the carvings. The Nazca lines are not deep, you discover. Two or three inches of red stones have been neatly removed to form the line of the white earth underneath. What shape is this? You wonder. Like your Grandpa Jasper said, the image is not visible from a standing position.

Maybe if you walk it, you will figure it out?

You start to follow the Nazca line instead of continuing your search. It seems to be a large circle. As you walk and walk, you become certain, that you are traversing a huge spiral. It must be a quarter of a mile across. When you have walked many circles, and many miles, you finally arrive in the center. It has grown dark. You are famished and thirsty, but strangely peaceful. You look up at the stars popping out overheard. You turn to try to find a familiar constellation.

Turn to page 101.

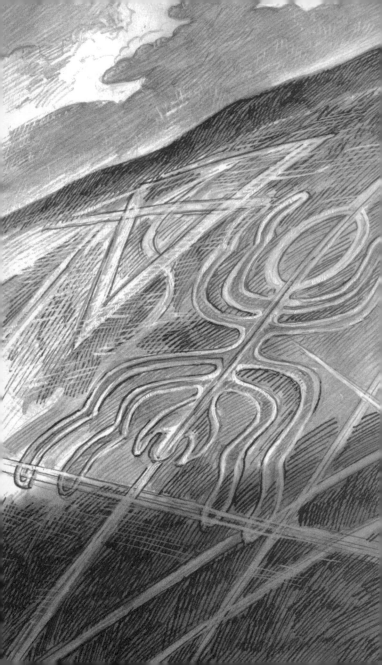

"Honey?" your mother cries. "Are you out there? It's dinnertime."

Your head snaps back and you look about. You are in the backyard of the ranch house. Lights from the kitchen stream out over your grandpa's vegetable garden. You breathe of sigh of relief. You're home!

The End

102

You turn around and run. The desert plain is flat and the stones are firm. You soon put some good distance between yourself and the Nazca carvers. But they do not give up and continue running after you. After fifteen minutes, you are gasping for breath. You look around. There's some sort of path that leads straight off the edge of this high plateau. You follow it. But unless you are willing to jump over 800 feet, it seems to end right there, at the edge.

"Psst!"

Go on to the next page.

You look over the cliff's edge and see a young girl. She has blonde pigtails and is wearing a wool dirndl.

"Who are you?" you cry in surprise. "And what are you doing here?"

"I took a wrong turn in the Labyrinthe. Whenever anyone shows up here on the Plains of Nazca, the locals think you're a god. The problem is that if you don't act like one, they like to kill you. Hop down! You'll be safe down on this ledge with me. The Nazca are terrified of heights." she replies. Then she adds, "My name is Elena."

You turn around and see 30 Nazca carvers running toward you, waving their arms and yelling. You look back down at Elena. There's not much choice.

So you jump

Turn to page 104.

104

You land and almost fall over the edge but Elena grabs you just in time.

"This way," she says, pointing to an indentation in the cliff. "It's an overhang. No one can see you from above."

"What's the Labyrinthe?" you ask.

Elena cocks her head to the side. "You don't know what the Labyrinthe is? Then how did you get here?"

"It's a long story. I started out in New Mexico a day ago. I seemed to go back in time somehow. I touched a petroglyph on the wall of a boxed canyon on my family's ranch."

"So you found the Labyrinthe by accident!" Elena exclaims. "That's terrific!"

"But I am still not sure what it is," you say.

"The Labyrinthe is a web of caves that lead to trails of time inside the Earth. There are secret openings of the Labyrinthe in most places around the world. But they are hidden. You just need to know how to find them," she replies.

Turn to page 106.

106

You notice a small crevice in the rock wall behind where Elena stands.

"Does that lead to the Labyrinthe?" you ask, pointing.

"Yes, it does." she says.

"And how does it work once you're inside?" you persist.

"It's just like one of those Choose Your Own Adventure books," she answers. "You come to a fork in the paths, and you have to make a choice. Come on. I'll show you how."

She reaches out her hand and smiles. You reach your hand forward and grasp it.

The End

You grab the flaming torch, and head carefully up the left tunnel. You walk for several minutes as the tunnel twists and turns. Just as the torch flames begin to weaken, you come to another fresh torch attached to the side of the wall. You exchange torches and continue with a fresh flame. Four torches later, you feel cool air wafting toward you. It feels like you have walked miles. You turn one last corner and the tunnel opens up into a spectacular cavern. You hold the torch up and gasp at what you see.

The walls of the cave are covered in a herd of ancient horses. The flickering firelight makes it seems that they are moving.

But where are you? The only place you have heard of this type of cave painting is Europe.

Seconds later you are dumbfounded when a tour guide comes through leading a pack of Chinese tourists. Everyone exclaims and points–at you!

"What are you doing here?" the tour guide demands in a heavy accent.

Turn to page 110.

"Where's here?" you reply.

"This is Lascaux," he answers. "A UN World Heritage site. These are some of the finest cave paintings from the Upper Paleolithic period in the whole country of France."

"I'm in France?" you cry.

The tour guide is not amused. In a few minutes, some security guards escort you out of the cave and into the administration offices.

You're going to have a lot of explaining to do.

And how are you ever going to get back home to New Mexico?

The End

About the Illustrators

Gabhor Utomo was born in Indonesia. He moved to California to pursue his passion in art. He received his degree from the Academy of Art University in San Francisco in spring 2003. Since his graduation, he has worked as a freelance illustrator and has illustrated a number of children's books. Gabhor lives with his wife Dina and his twin girls in the San Francisco Bay Area.

Vladimir Semionov was born in August 1964 in the Republic of Moldavia, of the former USSR. He is a graduate of the Fine Arts Collegium in Kishinev, Moldavia, as well as the Fine Arts Academy of Romania, where he majored in graphics and painting, respectively. He has had exhibitions all over the world, in places like Japan and Switzerland, and he is currently Art Director of the SEM&BL Animacompany animation studio in Bucharest.

About the Author

R. A. Montgomery has hiked in the Himalayas, climbed mountains in Europe, scuba-dived in Central America, and worked in Africa. He lives in France in the winter, travels frequently to Asia, and calls Vermont home. Montgomery graduated from Williams College and attended graduate school at Yale University and NYU. His interests include macroeconomics, geopolitics, mythology, history, mystery novels, and music. He has two grown sons, a daughter-in-law, and two granddaughters. His wife, Shannon Gilligan, is an author and noted interactive game designer. Montgomery feels that the new generation of people under 15 is the most important asset in our world.

**For games, activities, and other fun stuff,
or to write to R. A. Montgomery,
visit us online at www.cyoa.com**

COLLECT THEM ALL!

CHOOSE YOUR OWN ADVENTURE 1

THE ABOMINABLE SNOWMAN

CHOOSE FROM 28 ENDINGS!

BY R. A. MONTGOMERY

COLLECT THEM ALL!

CHOOSE YOUR OWN ADVENTURE 3

SPACE AND BEYOND

CHOOSE FROM 42 ENDINGS!

BY R. A. MONTGOMERY

CHOOSE YOUR OWN ADVENTURE® 6
HOUSE OF DANGER
CHOOSE FROM 20 ENDINGS

COLLECT THEM ALL!

CHOOSE YOUR OWN ADVENTURE® 7

RACE FOREVER

CHOOSE FROM 33 ENDINGS!

BY R. A. MONTGOMERY

CHOOSE YOUR OWN ADVENTURE® 9

LOST ON THE AMAZON

CHOOSE FROM 28 ENDINGS!

BY R. A. MONTGOMERY

COLLECT THEM ALL!

CHOOSE YOUR OWN ADVENTURE® 13

THE CLASSIC SERIES IS BACK!
CHOOSE FROM 23 POSSIBLE ENDINGS.

CUP OF DEATH

BY SHANNON GILLIGAN

COLLECT THEM ALL!

COLLECT THEM ALL!

CHOOSE YOUR OWN ADVENTURE® 32

THE CLASSIC SERIES IS BACK!
CHOOSE FROM 20 POSSIBLE ENDINGS.

U.N. ADVENTURE:
MISSION TO MOLOWA

BY RAMSEY MONTGOMERY